WHEN DEATH TOUCHES YOU

Why Private Writing Heals & Resolves Leftover Issues
A GUIDE

by

Marilyn J. Walker, Ph.D.

authorHOUSE™

1663 LIBERTY DRIVE, SUITE 200
BLOOMINGTON, INDIANA 47403
(800) 839-8640
WWW.AUTHORHOUSE.COM

First published by AuthorHouse 08/24/04

ISBN: 1-4184-1112-4 (e)
ISBN: 1-4184-1113-2 (sc)

Library of Congress Control Number: 2004105025

Printed in the United States of America
Bloomington, Indiana

This book is printed on acid-free paper.

Acknowledgements

Throughout the years, many trusted me with their innermost thoughts and feelings, some of which are included anonymously herein. I am humbled and grateful.

To those who critiqued, edited or proofread the manuscript along the way, your thoughts and suggestions are invaluable gifts. Thank you.

I also appreciate friends and family, near and far, who encouraged me to finish this work.

Dedication

Dear Mama and Daddy,

Our family singing around the piano is a sweet memory. Remember, "Swing Low, Sweet Chariot?"

I looked over Jordan, and what did I see?
. . . A band of angels coming after me,
Coming for to carry me home. . .

If you get there before I do,
. . . Tell all my friends I'm coming, too . . .

You got there first, but I'll take my turn when the time is right. This book is dedicated to your memory with love.

Preface

Dear Reader,

When death touches you, it is no longer a remote concept. It is very personal, and sets off a kaleidoscope of emotions. We don't all react according to predetermined "steps." Disturbing emotions can lie dormant – we don't consciously realize they are even there – and then emerge weeks, months, or years later.

Writing (in private – not to be read by anyone but you) is a powerful catharsis. Herein are guidelines designed to help you face what you must, and then write your way toward peace and hope – after the initial period of shock and grief is over.

Relief can emerge through your own fingertips as you are guided to:

- Deal with leftovers from the immediate aftermath;
- Address what happened;
- Consider unanswered questions;
- Actively grieve;
- Ease tension in the family;
- Purge blocked emotions (hurt, blame, anger, guilt or shame);
- Remember joy; and
- Reinvest in love.

Life is hard, and dying inevitable, but life is for the living. You need not envision yourself as an author to use pen or keyboard to release disturbing emotions and discover a renewed zest for life through private writing.

Come with me. The guidelines within show you how. Skip the sections that do not apply to you, and choose from the table of contents whatever is most needed at a given time.

Marilyn J Walker, Ph.D.

Table of Contents

PART I:
FACING THE REALITY
OF DEATH

Marilyn J. Walker, PH.D

Chapter 1: The Initial Impact

When death touches us, we are forever changed. We struggle with a variety of emotions as we face a future without those we had expected to share it with and, for a brief moment, we become sharply aware of our own inevitable demise.

Relationships are of central importance to most of us and the loss of one brings inestimable sadness. Even with belief in an afterlife, it is hard to view physical death as a glorious transformation into spirit. The end of dreams for this life, especially for those who die young, creates stinging disappointment.

1) Do only what you must do.

Shock and grief temporarily interfere with our ability to plan the future wisely. While you are hurting so much in the immediate aftermath of a death, make no major decisions:

· Don't plan to move or put the house up for sale at this time.

· Give nothing away, whether a car, ring, or anything else. There may be some who want this or that, or think they should have it. Soon after someone's death is not the time to

3

consider what is reasonable, feasible or fair. Tell anyone who asks, to wait until you are in a better frame of mind to think about material things.

- Shock can usually get you through performing various tasks related to death, from the most unpleasant to the mundane. Decisions regarding funeral arrangements, memorial services etc., have to be made. Even if the deceased had done some pre-planning, family and friends should be notified, some of whom may help you with contacting others or in last-minute decision making.

- Funeral/memorial arrangements range widely in cost. Spend only what you can afford. Counselors associated with funeral homes should be able to help you make choices that are tasteful and meaningful without trying to "talk you up to a higher level of cost" that will take years to pay off. Experiences of others in your community who have lost loved ones can be useful in selecting whose services to use.

- You will need multiple certified copies of the death certificate. Ask the City Registrar in the city or town where the death occurred. You may obtain additional copies at any

time, but to avoid delay and further inconve-
nience (privately made copies are not accept-
able), it is wise to obtain a separate one for
each of the following purposes:

1) Settling insurance claims, one for each company: life insurance, mortgage insurance, auto/
accident insurance, and insured loans and
credit cards

2) Transfer of checking and credit union accounts

3) Stocks or bonds account transfers, one for each
corporation

4) Entry into bank deposit vaults

5) Social Security benefits

6) Welfare benefits

7) Veteran's Administration benefits

8) Railroad retirement benefits

9) Union benefits

10) Transfer of real property: houses, lots

11) Title transfer for each automobile, boat,
camper or trailer

12) If required, to qualify for time off from work
for bereavement

13) Any requested copies for children or other family members

2) **Seeking tranquilizing medication.**

If intense pain or depression continues, see a physician. Most of them are experienced in what works best, and are empathetic. This is ordinarily a short-term aid. If you find yourself becoming dependent on medication, try to locate a specialist or program to help you explore how to wean yourself off.

Chapter Two: Beginning to Write

Few people have experience in writing about feelings. Remember, no one need see it but you, and writing is a powerful catharsis. To begin, just write something down – "okay, here I go" – or draw a heart, just anything that comes to mind. It may take several attempts before you are ready to write about your experience of loss. When you do start, you may want to write in stages, or at times when you have the luxury of indulging in private thoughts and memories.

1) **Title a journal with the name of the person whose death it will be about.**

Adjustment following a death can be wrenching, but previous experience from childhood on have taught us caution about exposing our feelings. We often shield them even from ourselves so that we can do what we must do. When asked how we are, we are likely to say, "Okay," when, in fact, we are hurting inside. Rediscovering the emotions we have suppressed and finding a safe way to express them outwardly is usually the beginning of healing.

Although the memory of those we love will always be with us, the trauma of their deaths can subside. Recounting our experiences and what we felt when death intruded can begin a catharsis so that, eventually, life can continue with some degree of normalcy. The following checklists will lead you step-by-step through death-related memories. This is important, because the repression of painful memories blocks grief as well as healing. Working through past emotions and gaining new insights will not totally eliminate the grief of loss, but your energy will not be siphoned off by the most debilitating emotions.

Using the outlines herein provided, make a journal, writing out an account of what happened. First, decide which death that has touched your life will be your focus. Each death will require going through the steps again.

For most people, the active expression of *writing* is more healing than *just thinking or speaking*. You aren't likely to be able to go through all of the steps at once or even within a brief time. If you are interrupted or become too distraught, take a break until you feel like working through some more. Be especially careful that you do not let any surfacing anger or depression trigger destructive impulses toward yourself or anyone else. The point is to heal, not be overcome. As your journal progresses, you may want to share the feelings that emerge with a trusted confidante who can provide any needed caution or comfort.

The lists that follow may elicit disturbing memories and intense feelings that come from the past and were "forgotten" – repressed – to protect you from them at that time. When they are retrieved, felt, and accepted, you begin a new journey to realize your optimal state of wellbeing.

·   What was the relationship between you (husband, wife, child, parent, friend, patient, crime suspect, stranger, etc.).

·   How old was s/he when s/he died?

·   How long ago was that?

·   How old were you?

2) What caused the death?

·   Illness (name it if you know).

·   Accident (describe it if you can).

·   Tornado, flood, earthquake, hurricane, or volcano.

- Homicide (name who killed him/her if you know).

- Suicide (write down anything you know about it).

- Terrorist attack.

- Riot or war.

- Don't know. After missing for _____, s/he was assumed dead.

3) Where did s/he die?

- In my arms, or next to me.

- At home.

- In the hospital.

- At an accident or crash site.

- At work.

- On a street or highway.

- In a lake or ocean.

- Field of battle.

- Other. You name it.

4) If you suspected death had occurred, how long was it before you knew for sure?

- Minutes

- Hours

- Days
- Weeks
- Months
- Years

When we are waiting to learn the fate of a loved one, the emotions evoked can be some of the worst traumas of our lives. Discuss in your journal all that apply.

5) What did you feel during that time of wait?

- Panic, anguish
- Hope
- Fear
- Numb
- Guilt
- Anger
- Other. You name it.

6) How did you finally find out?

- I was there.
- Got a phone call.
- I found the body.
- Someone came to get me.

·   Was contacted by police or the military.

·   Other. You name it.

7) What was your initial reaction?

·   Shock.

·   Nothing, numb, or dazed.

·   Disbelief.

·   Intense pain.

·   Relief that his/her suffering was over.

·   Anxiety or fear about the future.

·   Other. You name it.

8) Record all the duties you had to perform related to the death.

·   Dig through rubble of earthquake, tornado, fire, wreckage, etc.

·   Identify the body or remains.

·   Approve or deny autopsy.

·   Decide about organ donation.

·   Clean up blood or excrement.

·   Answer questions by investigators or reporters.

·   Notify others.

·   Obtain death certificate.

·   Arrange for burial, cremation, or vault.

·   Select urn, casket, tombstone, gravesite.

·   Plan funeral or memorial services.

·   Other. You name it.

Shock may prevent intense pain for a while, allowing us to function in a kind of emotional vacuum. Immediately after a death, necessary activities occupy our minds, and friends and family are generally around us. Later we are vulnerable to a roller-coaster of thoughts and feelings – at a time when we are likely to be alone.

10) What did you experience some time after the funeral or memorial services were over?

Write down all that you can remember, noting the ups and downs.

·   Love

·   Gratitude

·   Grief, sorrow

·   Loneliness

·   Fear

·   Pain

·   Anger

·   Resentment or blame

· Relief

· Regret

· Depression

· Guilt

· Shame

· Confusion

· Sleeplessness

· Physical symptoms: chest pain, stomachache, headache, etc.

· Other. You name it.

11) Record any reactions you can remember that were hard to accept or talk about

· Self-blame regarding the death.

· Hatred toward someone or organization.

· Relief that I was no longer burdened with caring for him/her.

· Shame that my loved one died while engaging in an illicit or illegal activity.

· Anger toward someone I believe to be at least partially responsible.

· Resentment about the distribution of the deceased's possessions.

· Bad feelings toward the one who died. Even when the relationship with the deceased was rocky or hurtful, grief can be intense. Regret for what could have been, but wasn't, can be as painful as the loss of someone who was a constant joy. Not only is the chance for reconciliation gone, but we may feel cheated of the years when understanding was not there. Writing about them may help you to resolve whatever is still bothersome, and find peace of mind. The following chapters show you how to do that. Meanwhile, I suggest engaging in ongoing remembrances or active grieving to help you accept the death, honor the spirit of the deceased, and speed the healing process (see *Chapter 5: Remembrances and Active Grieving).*

Marilyn J. Walker, PH.D

Chapter 3:
Unanswered Questions

Trying to get at the truth may not be easy. Following are some common questions, possible avenues to pursue for information, and perhaps some answers. Write your questions in the journal as well as how and what you learned, the sources or barriers to getting information, and how you feel about it.

1) How did s/he die?

Try to locate eyewitnesses to ask specific questions. Was s/he still alive when you saw him/her? Did s/he say anything? Talk to nurses or caretakers. If an autopsy was performed, request a report from the medical examiner. If your loved one was a member of the armed services, ask the military to help you find the facts. Get whatever medical information or records you can from attending physicians or hospital.

2) What caused the accident?

Ask to see official copies of accident reports from police, sheriff, or other office. If eyewitnesses or others that were present before, during, or after the tragedy can be located, they may know some-thing officials do not. Since conflicting reports are common, you may have to settle on one that seems most credible to you.

3) Could the illness or injuries have been prevented or cured?

Medical science (or physicians that you trust) may be able to shed light on your questions. If you learn that prevention or cure may have been pos-sible, you may be able to join with other voices advocating needed precautions. Proponents of various kinds of treatments may claim that some other approach would have been better than that which was used, but it would be hard to prove since all therapies from all schools of thought have both successes and failures.

4) Who killed him/her?

This is one of the most frustrating and some-times infuriating questions about a homicide. Law enforcement personnel often have few leads to follow or are overwhelmed with work. Over time, they will likely reduce efforts to find the perpetrator. Your continuous help in trying to uncover new evidence or information can encourage a more tenacious investigation. If you can find a clairvoyant with a record of success in helping law enforcement, they might help. Ask at various police agencies.

5) Why did s/he get killed in a place where s/he was supposed to be?

Question authorities of the school, church, workplace, or other locale you naturally assumed was safe. Knowing what safety measures were in place might help understand how it happened. Precautionary policies are generally strengthened after such deaths, although few places, if any, can be made 100% safe.

Even when experts' efforts to explain the motives of perpetrators ring true, the greater question of divine justice is left unanswered. That life isn't necessarily fair according to what we believe about deserving vs. not deserving is something most of us have to accept.

6) In the case of suicide, why did s/he do it?

This can be hard to fathom, even if a suicide note is left. Often no friend or family member suspected that stresses were becoming overwhelming. Discussions with the victim's friends or schoolmates may help put the pieces together. Sometimes owners of metaphysical bookstores can direct you to reliable psychic channelers or mediums who might make contact with the loved one's spirit. Have your questions ready, and be cautious. There are lots of wannabes and charlatans. Whether or not answers are found, self-blame is probably the most common reaction. It has little value unless some lesson is learned but, when that takes place, you need to release that feeling and move on (see *Chapter Eleven: Guilt and Shame*).

7) Why was s/he doing . . . whatever, knowing it was dangerous?

The behavior in question may have been discussed many times, but part of the human condition is the ability to feel indestructible, particularly when we are young. Sometimes the more dangerous an activity, the more exciting it becomes. Other times, the awareness of danger isn't enough to remove the enticement to do it. All of us make bad choices sometimes; it's just that usually they aren't fatal.

8) Did s/he suffer, or die quickly?

This can be a matter of conjecture. If the circumstances suggest the possibility of remaining alive for a time, suffering is a possibility. Again, eyewitnesses may be able to shed light on that question. Understand though, that suffering is relative. What brings intense pain to one may not to another. We all suffer at times for various reasons, and I continue to be amazed at how much physical and emotional pain humans can withstand. It is not pleasant to think of our loved one suffering, but it is quite possible that s/he became unconscious, numb with shock, or psychically lifted out-of-body. Find comfort in the fact that release came, and they suffer no more.

9) Is my loved one/friend alive as a spirit somewhere? If so, can I make contact?

A major tenet of most religions is that humans are endowed with souls that survive physical death. In addition, transcendent experiences of thousands upon thousands of individuals throughout history testify to the fact that the soul can separate from the body. Spiritual experiences are common and world-wide. Trying to convince persons who have had spiritual experiences that they did not have them can be as fruitless as persuading patients in pain that they really don't have any. Certainly spiritual experiences, as well as pain, can be imagined or faked, but to assume that *all* of the countless cases of spiritual incidents that have been reported throughout human history are hallucination or fraud is quite a stretch.

· Point of death visitations

The phenomena of seeing, hearing or sensing the presence of a deceased loved one is common. A telepathic message often accompanies the visit to the effect that, 'I'm okay; I love you.' When explaining the message, people typically say, 'I didn't actually hear a *voice,* but the message came inside my head.' Mental telepathy, a relay of information from one mind to another, seems to be the primary means of spiritual communication – quantum leaps ahead of phone, fax, or e-mail. That a loved one's soul has separated from the body, and survives in a spiritual realm, comes as a shock to some, though ultimately comforting.

· **Spiritual puzzles**

One of the puzzles among those who believe that the soul survives, is that among those who promised to make contact with friends or loved ones after death, few have done so. On the other hand, extrasensory, supernatural or telepathic communications to the living, both during sleep and awake states continue to be reported, as they have throughout history.

· **Channelers and Mediums:**
  Legitimate and Fraudulent

Some individuals with psychic sensitivities appear to be conduits between the living and spirits of the deceased. Two of the most trusted channelers at the time of this writing are Sylvia Brown and John Edwards. Unfortunately, there are many whose claims to psychic powers are rooted in greed or delusion. Step carefully.

* * *

Living with unanswered questions is part of the human condition; scientists, intelligence agents, explorers, detectives and philosophers spend their lives trying to answer them. If you exhaust every avenue trying to get the answers you seek, it is probably best for you to take a deep breath, and let it go. Invoking the two-word philosophy, "Oh, well," is sometimes the best we can do about unanswered questions and events that are outside our ability to control or explain.

Chapter 4:
Carrying on in Spite of Stress

It isn't always easy to do what we must do even under ordinary circumstances. Stress following a death can make it even more difficult.

1) **Physical symptoms. Which of the following did you experience?**

· Muscular tension.

· Increased heart rate

· Rise in blood pressure

· Irritability

· Depression, lethargy, low energy.

· Sleeplessness.

· Other.

What did you do to relieve the stress? How are you now?

2) **After losing a child.**

What is, or was most difficult and stressful?

· Adjusting to a routine without him or her.

· Quiet in the place of laughter, whining, noise, etc.

· Memories triggered by seeing his/her toys and clothes.

· Watching the child's siblings play without him/her.

· Sadness, loneliness, guilt, etc. of deceased child's brothers or sisters.

· Trying to answer when playmates ask where s/he is.

· Did either parent blame the other?

> *Our little boy drowned in the creek during a family outing. My husband and I each thought the other one was watching him and we both blamed each other. We came close to divorce.*

· Divorce. This sometimes follows the death of a child if one or both partners were staying in the marriage primarily for the sake of parenting, or if one blamed the other for the tragedy. In-laws tend to choose up sides according to whatever they believe about the issues between the couple. Wounded emotions can ripple through the family (see *Chapter 11: Hurt, Blame and Anger*).

· Recalled accusations from anyone that you weren't raising him/her just right: too strict or too lenient, too much or too little discipline, diet not ideal, etc.

Finding relief after the trauma of losing a child can be a long and arduous task. *Part IV: Remembering the Joy*, and *Part V: Reinvesting in Love* may help.

3) Death of husband, wife, fiancée or fiancé.

- Loss of companionship and emotional support (see *Part V: Reinvesting in Love*).

- Physical help with housework, childcare, yard maintenance, chauffeuring children, etc.

- Extreme adverse reaction by an infant or other child.

> *My son was only one year old when my husband died. Baby Danny sensed the anguish and stress around him and completely stopped eating. I finally had to hospitalize him.*

- Adjustment to different family routine.

- Changed plans for the future.

- Faced raising children alone.

> *After my husband died, I held on to the dreams we'd had together. It was many years before I was able to adjust to his death. In the meantime, I had three children to raise and just carried on the best I could.*

- Had to consider how to make a living or take over a business.
- Excluded from prior social groups.

Although it happens to men too, women particularly, if divorced or widowed, can find themselves no longer welcome among married friends. Persons feeling insecure in their marriages may view a suddenly single person as a threat.

- Propositioned by a married friend or relative.

It can be confusing when someone offers sex at a time you are hurting and in need of comfort. If you comply, you betray the trust of that person's spouse, adding more tension. If you don't, you have the added stress of wondering whether or not to reveal the offer to his/her spouse, and add new doubt about loyalty in relationships.

> *While growing up, I didn't know of any men among my relatives or neighbors that weren't loyal to their wives. After my husband died, I was hit on by so many married guys that I lost faith in men.*

- Sexual tensions.

Many find lovemaking comforting under agreeable circumstances. An initial attraction stemming from sexual urges may sour as the partners get better acquainted or circumstances make a liaison difficult. What tensions were relieved or worsened by involvement with a sexual partner?

· Relatives' disapproval of your dating or finding a new love interest.

The adage, "love is blind" is borne out over and over. Others may see what a vulnerable survivor may not. Listen well and step carefully. However, considering interest in a new love a betrayal of your previous mate is an unhealthy attitude (see Part *V: Reinvesting in Love*).

· Child's non-acceptance of your new romantic interest.

A child may want your time and attention focused on him/her, especially since the loss of the other parent. If the new person in our life is sensitive to this and is nurturing to the children as well as to you, it will go far in getting over this phase.

4) Loss of parent or grandparent.

What did you find most difficult?

· Loss of a primary confidante.

> *When my wife's mother was diagnosed with pancreatic cancer with only a few weeks to live, I was inconsolable. We were very close and I could talk to her about anything. Both my wife and I have positions where we supervise other people – we had to keep going.*

· Resentment among siblings over the privilege – or responsibility – of caring for the surviving parent or grandparent.

> *After my father died, my wife and I took turns helping my mother. We cleaned her house, took her shopping, and anything else she needed. None of my brothers or sisters would help, though they all lived close enough. But when she died, there they were, with their hands out, wanting her stuff.*

· Took remaining parent/grandparent into your home.

a)   What were the benefits – enjoyment of their company? Help with housework, children, or finances?

b)   If there was a downside, what was it – conflict over life style or child-rearing practices? Onset of dementia? Ill-will between your spouse and the elder?

- Moved to be near surviving parent/grandparent.

- Assisted remaining parent/grandparent financially, or in record keeping.

- Helped with estate planning, social security benefits, etc.

- Arranged for nursing care at home or in a care-taking facility.

- Other stresses resulting from the death of a parent/grandparent.

> *My grandmother died in a nursing home while I was away at college. It was hard to go to class or study because I hadn't been there to help her. One of my professors told me to write her a farewell letter – that from where she was, she'd know what was in my heart. I did that, and it helped, but I still felt guilty for a long time.*

5) Both parents.

- Reconciled their financial records, paying off any debt.

- Arranged for sale or rental of their home.

- Disposed of possessions.

- Had to deal with wrangling over the estate.

- Other.

6) Brother, sister, aunt, uncle, other relative or close friend.

· Who?

· What stresses were added to your life that made it harder to carry on?

7) Terrorism victims.

Deaths of others who are not necessarily family or friends can affect us dramatically. Record where you were when you learned of a terrorist strike, what stresses resulted, and how you coped.

· You were a professional or volunteer who helped dig in the rubble for victims.

· You took on more responsibility in a strategic facility (airport, utility plant, hospital, etc.).

· Gave mental or physical health care to survivors.

· Distress over social prejudice directed toward you or toward others.

· A kind of paralysis made it difficult to function.

· Changed plans out of fear of traveling on airlines.

· Was laid off due to cutbacks after terrorist attacks.

· Other.

8) Crime victims in neighborhood or work- place..

Record who was killed, how and where, and the stresses added to your life as a result.

> *When I was a teacher in a gang-infested area, some children found a dead body on their way to school. The kids were always revved up from shootings, threats and fights that took place regularly. I couldn't even begin to teach until I had calmed them down. How can you reassure kids they're safe when they're not?*

· You lived in high crime area: lots of shootings and stabbings. Some anxiety was a way of life.

· Acquaintance killed at bank or store by armed robber.

· Had extra security measures installed.

· Organized or participated in neighborhood watch

· Tried to prevent family member, friend or

neighbor from becoming a vigilante and taking "justice" into their own hands.

- Avoided local business place for fear of another hold-up.

- Took longer alternate route to avoid high-crime neighborhood.

- Arranged escort for children to get to school.

- Other.

Chapter 5:
Remembrances and
Active Grieving

Individual differences are vast, and each of us must choose what best may bring us solace. Remember to write in your journal what you do or did about your sorrow, and how that makes/made you feel. If you did not engage in any remembrance activity, try to explain to yourself why not, and consider doing it now.

1) Setting aside certain times to focus on your loss.

We are emotional beings – acknowledge and accept your feelings, whatever they are.

If tears come, let them come. Nothing can replace the catharsis of weeping.

2) Accepting comfort offered by friends and family.

Compassionate understanding or a hug can soothe as well as energize. Don't be afraid to ask – most will feel honored if you do, and will try to help.

3) Associating with others who mourn.

Meetings designed for survivors to help and

support each other can be found through help lines, the yellow pages, hospitals, social services, churches, synagogues, or other religious groups. It may be useful to ask others what they are doing or thinking, and in what ways they are coping or reaching out to others.

4) Utilizing rituals.

Participate in memorial services, say prayers, light candles, place flowers at the gravesite, knowing full well s/he is not there, but likely sees your loving attention from a higher plane. Lovingly care for the absent loved one's living quarters or prized possessions until you are ready to convert them into use by the living.

5) If the body was cremated, strewing the ashes in a meaningful location.

Select a rose garden, lake, ski slope or other place that held special meaning to your loved one (many places have ordinances restricting where ashes may be strewn). Make this a special occasion, celebrating the life of the departed. Try to find comfort in knowing that to become one with the earth is the ultimate fate of all physical forms, and that from death comes life.

6) Creating a home memorial.

Arrange photographs, flowers, icons of your religious faith, or favorite possession of the loved one in a special place. Leave it until it is no longer needed. For some, it may be when ready to more fully accept his/her place in a spiritual, non-physical realm. For others it may be when focusing more on remembered joy, at which time a photograph of the loved one doing what s/he loved to do may be placed in a special spot.

7) Arranging for a public memorial.

A plaque can be placed on a chair, wall, or by a tree planted in his/her honor.

Make a donation to an organization or institution for a building, stadium, etc. to be built in the name of your loved one.

8   Writing a note or letter to the deceased.

Assume s/he can see and understand it. Say what you want them to know. If need be, then destroy it to keep it private.

9) In a quiet room, imagining the deceased in a chair across from you.

Talk to him/her. Say "thank you," "I'm sorry," "I forgive you," "I love you," or anything else you want to communicate.

10) Practicing appreciation of his/her life as well as mourning the death.

Remember and talk about the sweet moments, fun, hopes and dreams (see *Part IV: Remembering Joy*).

11) Talking naturally about the deceased.

This helps adjust to the reality of death, relieves others who worry about you or who also mourn, and reduces discomfort for those uncertain of what to say to you.

12) Engaging in activities that assist others in some way.

Help raise funds to provide a scholarship for a child, or to support organizations that fight drunk driving or drug use. Join movements or demonstrations to help prevent future deaths from the cause that took your loved one/s. The good that has been done by bereaved survivors, in their desire to help others, is inestimable. It is one way to ensure that the loved one's death will in some way be of use to the living.

The internet and yellow pages can help you locate organizations or existing groups you may wish to support. Be careful, though. Unscrupulous persons can prey on the bereaved for their own profit. Direct contact with a known institution is a safety measure.

13) Reinvesting love in others.
Whether you reach out to friends, family, children, or a romantic partner, giving and receiving love stimulates profound healing. Still being able to love is not a betrayal of the deceased but more likely a tribute to shared love (see *Part V: Reinvesting in Love*).

14) Practicing replacement of sorrowful memories.
Recurrent images of the death site, cemetery, etc. can prolong pain. As soon as possible, recall the joy, proud moments and successes of the deceased. Then, if you can, envision your loved one alive in a

peaceful spiritual realm without the trouble and anguish of mortal life. Beautiful paintings, hung where you can see them frequently, can bring comfort.

15) Distributing possessions that belonged to the deceased.

Consider survivors who will cherish them or others who can use them. Whether sold or given away, knowing that someone else is using an item that once belonged to your loved one can be gratifying.

Chapter 6: Terminal Diagnosis

All of us live with the prospect of certain death, but when an illness or injury is diagnosed as incurable and fatal, the emotional impact can be intense. You can be sure that you, or whomever has been thus diagnosed, will indeed die (since we all must), but when that will take place isn't so certain even with a prognosis of a few weeks or months to live. Medical breakthroughs continue to occur, and diseases can undergo "spontaneous remission" without explanation. If you have received a terminal diagnosis, consider the following.

1) **Getting another opinion from a different medical group.**

Even the most conscientious medical and technical personnel can make mistakes. Other times, times, in spite of great technological advances, tests that have been run leave the best professionals with only educated guesses.

2) **Considering what you yourself can do to improve your condition.**

If you become very weak, or suffer great pain or

anxiety, you may need to rely on another person to help you with diet, possible exercise, ways to rest, sleep or reduce tension.

Ask for help with finding out about current clinical trials of new treatments, and getting information about your condition from the internet.

3) Exploring participation in clinical trials of new treatments.

Ask your physicians to find out what studies are being done and where.

> *Mitchell, a veteran of the Gulf War, was diagnosed with Chronic Lymphocytic Leukemia, historically a fatal condition, with a prognosis of six months to live. He got his affairs in order but agreed to participate in a clinical trial of a new medication (STI 5-71) being conducted through the Veteran's Administration. Mitchell's leukemia is now in remission; he is back to full-time work; and enjoying his life. The medication had such success with participants that it was approved by the Federal Drug Administration for general use in 2001.*

4) **Searching the internet for information about conditions such as yours.**

You are likely to find the latest research findings, accounts of others coping with the same condition, and support groups.

5) **Investigating alternate forms of therapy: acupuncture, herbal remedies, therapeutic massage, chiropractic treatment, or healing rituals.**

Traditional medicine is probably the best choice, but other approaches sometimes succeed. If pursuing herbal remedies, make certain they will not interfere with pharmaceutical treatments. It is difficult to ascertain whether or not claims for various products or procedures being pitched have an authentic history of positive effects. Practitioners in alternate forms of therapy can be found in the yellow pages and may be able to answer many of your questions. A caring person can be comforting, whether or not s/he has the means to extend your life.

6) **Worry about becoming a burden.**
- You are uncomfortable that you need help.

These feelings are understandable and show a concern for others. It is often the case however, that caretakers enjoy what they do, and when they get a smile and a "thank you" for one they care for, it makes their day. That alone makes your care much less of a burden. If you are able, write regular "thank you" notes to them, or ask someone to write for you as you dictate. Bringing a bit of pleasure to someone else can make you feel less guilty for being dependent.

- The expense for your care is depleting family resources.

If your expenses are being paid from your money, that is an appropriate way for it to be used. If it comes in part or wholly from others, thank them. Financial sacrifice for the care of a loved one is honorable. Remember the old adage, "You can't take it with you," and neither can they. If your family has to struggle financially, so be it. Many families struggle even without medical or long term care expense. Writing them regular notes, thanking them for their help, will make their lives sweeter as well as yours.

7) Living until you die.

Focus on what you can do, not what you can't. As much as possible, engage in things that interest you and with friends and family.

8) Final arrangements.

Put bequeaths and requests in writing, including designations about future care and financial arrangements for pets. Get legal help to ensure the format and wording are clear, and challenges unlikely.

9) Trying to heal old hurts between you and others.

Most of our lives are not as peaceful as we would like, just as world peace has proved so far to be elusive. One of the best gifts one can leave behind is a deeper understanding and forgiveness of others. Then forgiving ourselves for our misguided errors, in both thought and action, can help us at least to die in peace. Discussion and techniques in *Part III: Effects of Blocked Emotions* may help.

10) Seeking help from hospice personnel.

The experience of emotional or physical pain can be lonely even when loved ones and health care professionals are trying their best to help. The hospice tradition is designed to make a dying person as comfortable as possible, physically and emotionally, whether one remains at home or in a hospice setting.

11) Making peace with God.

Seek the counsel of whatever spiritual advisor best represents your beliefs – priest, rabbi, minister, monk, or other wise person. Take whatever steps are necessary to make peace with God. Direct supplication – "God, have mercy on me. Forgive me my shortcomings and failures" is appropriate, in whatever stage of life we find ourselves. Bargaining with God to extend life until a certain date or special event occurs seems to be successful for many people. Countless times, one lives until after a wedding or graduation, or until a certain family member arrives.

12) Being open to spirit beings to help you cross over when the time comes.

Dying persons often see angels or spirits of relatives hover over them to accompany them to the spirit realm. Stories of family members and medical personnel who have also witnessed this phenomena are legion.

Chapter 7: Explaining Death to Children

1) When someone that the child loves, dies.

When a parent, important caregiver, close family member or classmate dies, a child's world is rocked. A child can appear stoic or undisturbed on the surface, and still feel confused, frightened or abandoned. It is central to their wellbeing for adults in their lives to follow the steps outlined below.

If you lost a loved one when you were a child, write in your journal which of the steps below were or were not done with you, and how it affected you. If you were the one trying to explain death to a child, record what you did and the child's apparent reaction. If you skipped a step, it is never too late to try to set things right. Then record that too.

· Reassurance about their own physical safety.

· Who will take care of them.

· Explain why the death took place within limits of the child's understanding.

· Where the loved one is now – both body and spirit – and why s/he can't come back.

- If the child reports a dream about the deceased loved one or mentions seeing him/her, accept it as fact. The phenomena of the spirit of a deceased person appearing to the still living is common. Suggest that the loved one was just coming to say s/he's okay now, that s/he loves you, and to say goodbye.

- Explain that life is full of changes and dangers, and that eventually death comes to everybody. It is important though, to emphasize how important it is to be careful and take good care of themselves so they can grow up, learn lots of things, have their own families, and to do whatever they can to make the world a better place.

- Let children know what happened and the cause of death. Explain how best to protect themselves. For example, if someone died in an automobile accident, talk about what can be done to greatly reduce the odds of having one. If needed, reassure the child so that s/he does not become afraid of riding in a car, bus, plane, etc.

- Before giving a religious explanation, make clear the physical cause of death.

Spiritual beliefs that may comfort an adult can be frightening to a child. The following is such a case.

> *An eight-year-old boy with symptoms of severe anxiety was referred to me. He could not focus on his schoolwork and was afraid to go to sleep. I learned that he was fearful of God. He remained hyper-vigilant so he could run and hide if a big arm reached down to grab him. He had been told that God loved his little brother so much, that He took him up to Heaven to be with Him. The child hadn't been told that his brother died of an illness that my young patient did not have. When the physical cause of the brother's death was explained, the boy's anxiety began to recede.*

· Speak naturally about the deceased. Ask children questions from time to time.

> *Remember when Grandpa gave you this toy?*
> *Do you ever dream about Grandma?*
> *What do you miss most about your brother?*

· Speak of the loftiest actions and attitudes for which the deceased loved one/s will be remembered. In helping children prepare to make the most of life, whatever good examples can be held before them can help deter bad choices all too available to them as they are growing up.

· Ask lots of questions to help the child articulate his/her own thoughts and feelings.

2) If a Child's Own Death is Pending

If death seems imminent, prepare yourself and the child for what is to come. Keeping notes in a daily journal can help you focus on what is most important to do, release emotional tension, and remain tranquil.

· Help the child understand what is wrong and what is being done to try to correct it.

· Encourage the child to accept whatever medicines or procedures are designed for his/her benefit or comfort.

· It may not be necessary or possible for the child to know that s/he could soon die, but it can be useful to explain that all people must die some time. Comment that if s/he dies before you, you will see him/her in the spirit world when your time comes. Children with terminal illnesses are able to accept the prospect of death with surprising calm.

- Continue to express unconditional love and encouragement even when there is every indication that the child is unconscious. Countless people have later reported that they "heard" everything going on even while in a coma or under anesthesia.

- Let the child know that one or more angels may come to help him/her when the time comes.

- Sometimes when all efforts to heal a dying child have been unsuccessful, a child will endure suffering and struggle to stay alive so as not to make the loved ones sad. If, in your judgement, this is the case, tell him/her its okay to go be with the angels, that you will be okay. As the beloved face relaxes into a peaceful letting go, you will know that you have given a gift of love.

Marilyn J. Walker, PH.D

PART II:
TENSION IN THE
FAMILY

Marilyn J. Walker, PH.D

Chapter 8: How a Death Affects Old Animosities

Whatever discord there is in a family or work group, a death can help to heal, or make it worse. Habitual misunderstandings, jealousy, and competition for the approval and affection of other group or family members can be particularly keen following a death.

Rivalry is part of the human condition. Children vie with each other for parental attention and approval. How much nurturing is required to avoid a fragile ego and jealousy toward others differs from one child to another. Ordinarily, those who have received continuous understanding and loving guidance are most likely to consider others with compassion, regardless of the circumstance.

Most individuals can recall one or more instances of unfairness, but do not develop an *attitude* that follows them through life. If memories of having wronged someone else surface while probing the past, consider what amends can be made.

Enlightened parents don't consciously favor one child over another, but it can happen. Also, the variations of sibling rivalry that evolve into patterns of contempt are common.

1) **Conflicts that most distressed you.**

- Write the names of those involved. Avoid fanning the flames of discord by taking precautions to prevent those persons from reading what you write.

- What issues were in dispute?

- How long has this gone on?

- How were you affected by it?

- As far as you know, how did it start?

- What did each one say, or believe about the other?

- How did each one think it should be re-solved?

2) **How the conflict showed up after the death.**

- Complaints about who was notified and when.

- Disagreement regarding the funeral, services, etc. Explain.

- Snide comments were made regarding the deceased or one of the survivors.

- Claims on the deceased's assets or possessions.

- Other.

- How did you feel about the discord?

3) Efforts to try to negotiate peace.

· Who tried to be peacemakers?

· Were there two opposing "camps?"

· What were the main contentions of each?

· What was your attitude toward each side?

Marilyn J. Walker, PH.D

Chapter 9: The Emotional Meaning of Possessions and Assets

When disputes arise over estates or personal items, it generally involves more than simple greed. Money or property items may symbolize one's importance to the deceased, or a special place within the group or family. Rivalries, unresolved expectations, and hurts that may have festered for years often emerge as desires for something from the deceased's estate.

1) Carrying out wishes of the deceased.

· Were his/her wishes known? Was there a will? If not, what is believed and why?

· If known, were the wishes carried out?

· How reasonable or fair do you think those wishes were? If not, why not?

· Were there legal disputes in which attorneys were used? If so, what was the outcome?

2) Your own feelings about the deceased's possessions.

· Many survivors say that when their loved

one died, a part of them died too, and they are reluctant to go on. Was this, or is this true of you?

- Do you sometimes feel guilty for being alive when the other is dead?

- Does the thought of giving away, selling or throwing away a loved one's possessions feel like a betrayal?

- To avoid pain, do you delay clearing out the deceased's living/work space or possessions? If so, this is understandable. The thought of parting with a beloved doll, Teddy bear or basketball following the death of a child can evoke unbearable sadness. It may take a while to face decisions about lovingly hand-made quilts, an unfinished novel or other pos-sessions of a parent or spouse.

- Is the loved one's room "just as s/he left it?"

- Is there still a place set at the table for him/ her? If yes, does seeing the unused plate, etc. make you sad, or bring you comfort?

- Do you expect to eventually clean out the deceased's office or living quarters, and

Make decisions about his/her possessions? If
yes, consider facing it. Until you do, a cloud
of unfinished business hangs over you.

**3) Possessions of the deceased that are still
in your care.**

- Papers: will, correspondence, memoirs,
documents.

- Monetary: bank accounts; trust funds; etc.

- Household goods.

- Lawn & patio furniture.

- Tools, weapons, or equipment.

- Vehicles.

- Personal items: jewelry, clothing, trophies,
toys.

- Other.

4) Choices and steps.

- How could space previously utilized by a
lost loved one be utilized for the living? An
extra guest room? A work room?

- Which one or more items do you want to
keep as a special memorial?

- What object or item of clothing are you
willing to dispose of now?

- How many can you try to dispose of per day?

It gets easier day by day.

- Have you asked relatives and friends if there is any item among the deceased's undesignated possessions they want? Does a granddaughter want that locket she admired? A nephew who likes fixing things, the tool kit?

- How do you feel about trying to sell any items that are left?

- To what charity might you donate certain items?

Chapter 10: Helping to Heal

It is a rare family or group – if one exists at all – that doesn't have lingering mistrust, rivalry, or resentment between some of its members. Family feuds are extremely difficult to defuse. Feelings run deep, and each person tends to believe his/her view of things is right. It is difficult for any of us to consider how things might look to others, having rehearsed our own view numerous times in our minds.

1) **Record your attitude regarding the animosities.**

   · Prefer to ignore them, and why.

   · You are engaged in the conflict. Explain how.

   · You would like to help heal the rift, if possible.

If you wish to be a peacemaker, you must exhibit continuous kindness, initiate delicate inquiry, and then listen thoughtfully to each one without jumping on their bandwagon. This is difficult for any of us. Listening is one of the most important skills we can develop, and yet is a rare occurrence. Three common factors prevent us from really listening to one another. We are most likely to interrupt someone who is trying to gain our understanding when we:

a) Aren't really interested;
b) Have already established strong views; chosen sides; and/or
c) Feel a need to be heard ourselves.

2) Who just won't listen.

Most of us can't, won't, or don't know how to listen well. Recall anyone who does any of the following when you're trying to make a point, and then evaluate your own habits:

· Interrupts.
· Keeps watching TV, reading, doing her nails, etc.
· Starts arguing before you've finished a sentence.
· Rolls their eyes, conveying "Here we go again," or
· Agrees just to get you to shut up, "Yeah, sure."

3) Thoughtful vs. dysfunctional listening.

A peacemaker must be able to listen thoughtfully. The following guidelines can help you evaluate yourself. What do you think you most need to practice?

· Listen without interrupting.

· Re-state what you hear to ensure you're not misunderstanding.

· Ask the other person if what you heard is what s/he meant.

· Gently ask for further explanation.

  How long have you felt this way?
  What exactly happened? How did it start?
  Do you believe s/he loved you? Why, or why not?
  What would make you feel better?
  Do you think you could start to ease the tension if you wanted to?

4) Trying to understand.

The admonition that we should not criticize until we have walked in another's shoes is easier said than done. Difficult as it may be, we must imagine how it would feel walking their path, or being inside their skin, if we have any hope of understanding.

5) When to speak, when not to speak.

Anyone is more likely to listen to us if we take time to listen to their explanations and try to understand their feelings. If someone in your life just won't listen, start listening thoughtfully to *them.* Then, before you make comment or suggestion, ask the other person if they would like to hear your thoughts on the matter. If they say yes, proceed with caution. If they say no, say nothing.

* * *

If your efforts can help purge negative feelings, perhaps from the safe haven of your understanding, one or another may be able to consider how things could have seemed to others. A simple, "I think now I understand how you could feel that way," goes a long way toward healing. Although it sometimes takes years before a chronic resentment can be fully released, civility can replace snide interchange. At the very least, you can make a concerted effort not to feed into the escalation of animosities.

PART III: EFFECTS OF BLOCKED EMOTIONS

Unbeknown to us, anger, hurt, and erroneous conclusions from our past can motivate inappropriate responses to current events. As time goes on, hurtful memories act as emotional splinters that fester like infected wounds inside us. Our physical health and feelings of self-worth can be adversely affected. Subconscious feelings consume energy, and can cause us to subtly radiate a negative aura. To free us from their contaminating effect on ourselves and others, we can cleanse them by retrieving, accepting, and expressing them.

Shock and necessary activities following a death can numb emotions, suppressing grief so that we can do what we must do. As time goes on, however, to feel our best and be able to live lovingly, we need to address our inner being, and, so to speak, launder our psyches.

Marilyn J. Walker, PH.D

Chapter 11: Hurt, Blame and Anger

Residues of hurt, blame or anger lurk within awareness *or* in our subconscious minds until they somehow are released. Such feelings may be toward the deceased, any other person or God.

It is doubtful that any relationship can be totally free from momentary or chronic hurt. Our expectations of intimate friends and family members far exceed those for casual acquaintances or work associates, and disappointment regarding them can be lingering and intense. Hurt, blame and anger are closely associated, sometimes intertwined. Anger toward God is not unusual.

1) **Writing notes or letters as a healing exercise.**

For some reason, writing letters (not to be mailed) can help recall emotions, clarify them and ultimately have a healing effect. It may seem silly to consider writing a letter to someone and not mail it, or to a deceased person or to God, but its benefit is

71

for *you*. Our physical health can be affected by blocked emotions. Suppressed feelings continue to affect our reactions, albeit not with our knowledge or consent.

Countless relationships are jeopardized because of unhealed experiences from the past. Exhuming our feelings and releasing negative ones can protect us from distorted thoughts in current relationships. Resentments that seem to be logical may actually be remnants from the past, as an objective observer would suspect.

Talking about feelings to an understanding person can be comforting, but writing them directly to whomever you feel them toward, using pen or keyboard, and seeing them on paper or screen, is a more powerful catharsis. It helps to read them back, add and revise as many times as necessary, until a feeling of release is accomplished. At that point, you may want to shred them and throw them away.

2) **Willingness to try.**

This letter-writing technique is harder than it sounds. Most people cannot do it at first. The effort brings up too many painful feelings that are hard to re-live, and some that we ourselves disapprove of. That is okay. There is no time schedule; let it unfold as you are ready. You may also want to make numerous revisions. Your feelings will likely change – becoming more intense, or softening – as you re-read and alter each draft.

3) **Expressing hurt, blame or anger to the deceased.**

There is almost always *some* left-over negative emotions when loved ones die that can haunt us for years. We may feel angry toward them for dying, or for being where they were – mountain climbing, on a lake, driving drunk, or at a party, etc. Following are some possible ways to begin explaining feelings that still linger.

- *Dear . . .*
- *I am sad and disappointed that I am left alone.*
- *I felt hurt/angry when I found out that . . .*
- *I could never understand why . . .*
- *I wish you could have . . .*
- *Maybe you did what you did because . . .*
- *Just want you to know that . . .*

· *There were times that I felt like –*
  (whapping) – you.

Knowing that nobody else is going to read what we write, we can be surprised at how vehement our feelings are. They may be difficult to write about because there is a commonly held idea that one shouldn't speak ill of the dead that may extend to writing angrily *to* the dead. Not all memories of deceased persons are laden with love or longing, however. When an abusive spouse dies, for example, one may feel relief instead of grief. When you express your feelings honestly, without having to put on a good face for others, a catharsis begins. If you felt like smacking that person, say so. Following are suggested issues you might want the deceased to understand:

· *I wish you could have been more caring*
  about . . .
· *When you – did whatever – it made me feel . . .*
· *It was honestly a relief when you died.*
· *Sometimes I thought about what I'd like to*
  do to you.
· *One thing I appreciated about you was that . . .*

- *Thank you for . . .*
- *I'm sorry if I . . .*
- *I forgive you; I love you.*

It may be a good idea ***not*** to let anyone see your writing. Some folks don't understand that physical expression can be healing. They might shake their heads or roll their eyes at you. Also, it's nobody's business but yours. If you would be more comfortable, you can tear up your writing. Perhaps burning it can be part of a purging ritual. If there is some possibility that your writing could be found and bring hurt to a still living person, destroy it to ensure that doesn't happen.

You might want to share your writing with a wise confidante who can understand the myriad emotions humans can have. It can be comforting to have such understanding expressed to you, and relieve whatever guilt you harbor for feeling what you feel.

Rather than destroy what you have written, you may want to keep the writing for a while to review it, add to it, or change it. Re-reading at a later time what you have previously written can help you keep track of how much you have healed or developed further understanding.

Sometimes more life experience causes us to temper our attitudes so that we gain a new under-standing of difficulties the deceased person faced, allowing us finally to forgive. When we are able to remember sweet memories, the new insight may be accompanied by regret that we weren't wiser when younger. However, since we are developmental creatures, we must reconcile ourselves to this human condition. Forgiving ourselves is important, though, and is addressed in the section on guilt and shame.

4) Anger/blame toward another person.

Anger toward those deemed responsible for a loved one's death is normal. Blame and anger toward an innocent person – a driver couldn't see a child run out in front of the car – is still normal.

Waiting for a trial of persons suspected of perpetrating a crime that directly or indirectly led to the death is an added frustration. Most of us want to see justice done, and the wheels of the courts turn slowly.

Writing letters – not to be mailed or delivered –
to anyone involved, expressing your feelings can be
a relief for you. Holding feelings in can be like a
cancer eating away. Below are some starting phrases
that may help you write.

· *To . . . (name anyone you believe is responsible for, or contributed to, the death).*

· *How could you . . .*

· *S/he was such a . . . person, and because
of you . . .*

· *Those of us who loved him/her feel . . .*

· *I think what should happen to you is . . .*

An example follows.

> *To the boy who killed our son in a drive-
by shooting: "You're still out there some-
where you cowardly little shit. Not enough
evidence to indict they say. I hope you
get shot in just the same way and rot in
Hell."*

· *When I think of you, and what you did, I feel
like . . .*

It's hard for those of us who grew up believing
in forgiveness to admit wishing harm toward another

person. Ultimately, we are healthier to forgive, but only after purging ourselves of blame and anger. To pretend forgiveness may be a prelude to actually doing so, but keeping dark emotions inside siphons off energy, lessening our ability to engage in a satisfying life.

> *Some time ago I lost a pet through the negligence of a vet. I was hurt and furious at the time. Instead of ranting and raving, I wrote a beautiful remembrance of all the characteristics of the dog that I so loved. I still have that eulogy and I treasure it.*

Residual anger can consume us. For a few, expressing negative feelings can become a *rehearsal,* increasing their intensity rather than serving as a catharsis. The goal is to release feeling, not to be overcome. Plotting actual revenge ultimately hurts you and adds another thorn to a society already torn by crime and violence. If anger keeps building, you should seek a specialist in anger management. A psychiatrist can prescribe calming medication if needed. Other counselors – psychologists, social workers – may initiate therapy that can help you find a healthy emotional balance.

5) Writing to God.

Sincere belief in God may include the expectation that if one is good – tries to follow the commandments, goes to worship services, prays, etc. that God will protect and reward. An unexpected death can throw such faith into tumult.

One begins learning at an early age that life isn't necessarily fair. The daily news reminds us that bad things can happen to good people. When a death touches us, however, it is a very personal and subjective experience. *"Why me?"*

Anger toward God needn't erode one's basic belief in Him, although we may have to rearrange our understanding of the relationship between God, humanity, life and death. You may have to give yourself permission to question God before writing to Him. Nursing a grudge won't provide answers to such basic questions, but expelling blame and anger can free us to seek them. Suggested phrases to begin a letter to God follow:

· *Why did You let this happen?*
· *I have tried hard to . . .*

- *I believed for so long that God is love; now I am confused, hurt and angry . . .*

- *If there is some good that can come of this death, please reveal it to me.*

- *You didn't protect him/her on earth; can I believe s/he is safe with You now?*

- *Dare I believe that I will see him/her again after this life?*

- *Please help me understand.*

- *Have mercy on me and grant me peace.*

- *Help me restore my faith, so I do not become embittered.*

- *Grant me grace to accept what comes, and continue life with a loving heart.*

Chapter 12:
Guilt and Shame

1) Regrets.

It is never too late to address interpersonal leftovers. It is common to regret words or acts directed toward a deceased person, or have remorse for real or perceived neglect of them.

A student, trying to hold back the tears, sought counsel in my university office following the unexpected death of his grandfather.

> *"My grandfather and I argued at our last meeting and the next week he dropped dead of a heart attack."*

The grandson's sorrow was not only because he lost a grandparent he dearly loved, but for the impatient words they had exchanged. I suggested he write a letter to his grandfather expressing all that was on his mind and in his heart – how much he loved him; how sorry he was for their misunderstanding, etc. When he did so, he found enough peace of mind that he could resume his studies.

Rarely are our hopes and dreams fully realized for our relationships. Part of our grief may be, "I wish I had told him . . ." Tell him now.

Writing such letters is a very personal affair. Because you are addressing a letter to someone who has died, some may think it strange. It is important, though, to write it *as if* the deceased can see it. If souls on the spiritual plane have deeper understanding than when in physical form, chances are your loved one already knows what you feel. No matter. Writing the letter is for *you*.

2) **Blaming one's self for the death.**

The ability to feel guilt is necessary to have an active, healthy conscience. However, it is often the case that when a death occurs, we tend to blame ourselves for events outside of our control.

> *"I shouldn't have let her use the car that night."*
> *"If only I had, or had not . . ."*

It is normal in retrospect to try and figure out what might have prevented a death. However, since we mortals are usually unable to foretell the future, the best we can do is try to make choices that seem safe at any given time. For example, it is reasonable to allow a responsible teenager to use the car for an agreed-upon purpose. Rule of thumb: if you considered the circumstances, and made a decision based on what most people safely do most of the time, you were being responsible. None of us can control the health and safety of our loved ones as much as we'd like, and we have to accept that fact along with whatever happens.

Culpability in someone's death isn't always easy to determine. A client told me:

> *"My mother and I fought all the time. She criticized me all my life. I wish she could have loved and accepted me. One day she was standing on a stool reaching for something and just keeled over and died. I had just screamed at her. I'm sure I caused her heart attack."*

This client intuitively knew that aside from whatever physical problems existed, her scream had *some* impact on her mother. Of course we humans affect each other's emotions, physical health, and ability to function. A new sadness was emerging in this young woman: that she did not better understand, and was not more compassionate while her mother was alive. This can be said of practically all humankind. We are developmental creatures; compassion and understanding do not come to us easily. As we grow older, we glean wisdom through life's lessons. Real insight, for most of us, comes partially through travail. This lady might have written:

- *I feel terrible that my screaming might have triggered your heart attack.*

- *Even if my scream didn't cause your heart attack, I feel rotten knowing that was the last thing you heard.*

- *I am having a hard time forgiving myself.*

- *If only I had known . . .*

- *I wish throughout our lives we could have . . .*

- *My scream came from years of not feeling loved or understood . . .*

- *Maybe if I understood better all the factors that made you like you were . . .*

- *Please forgive me for not trying harder to understand . . .*

- *I forgive you for . . .*

- *I hope you are at peace and that you can forgive me.*

3) Comments for health care professionals.

Whether your field is medical, EMS, nursing, psychology, etc., a certain degree of detachment is necessary for us to provide the best care possible. When one of our patients dies, however, regardless of the circumstance, it affects us emotionally. We ordinarily ask ourselves what we could have done differently, if anything, to prevent the death. We try to reconstruct what happened, considering fatigue, errors in medication or procedures, misinformation, or whether any one of the health care team was under the influence of drugs or alcohol.

A death or suicide of one of our patients reminds us of our limitations. As conscientious as we try to be, we can only do what is within our range of skill and knowledge, and we do sometimes make mistakes. Conducting a "case autopsy" to identify our mistakes or shortcomings, and what we have learned that can help improve our practices should be done privately, and then the notes destroyed.

Health care professionals are reluctant to admit errors of any sort, lest their practices or reputations suffer considerable harm. Filing damage suits is a lucrative industry for some attorneys. Whether a case is warranted or frivolous, defense lawyers try to keep damning information from the court, but it is wise to shred your note when finished. This would preclude any of your personal writing (if subpoenaed) being interpreted as "evidence" of neglect, or whatever, against you.

As a health care professional, you too may find that *personal writing* of notes or letters to the deceased can remove a splinter in your psyche. Try it. You may be surprised.

- *Dear . . .*
- *Thank you for trusting me to take care of you . . .*
- *I felt sad, disappointed, . . . when you died.*
- *I had hoped that . . .*
- *I believe what happened was . . .*
- *I will never forget you.*
- *Please forgive me for . . .*

4) When a death really was your fault.

If someone clearly died because of you – that is a terrible cross to bear. Write down what happened:

- Angry shove or strike.

- Negligence – no life preservers in the boat, left a child unsupervised in an area of obvious dangers, etc.

- Driving while under the influence of alcohol or drugs.

- Other.

Though bearing regret for whatever choices led to the death, writing a letter to the deceased can help ease your spirit. This will be difficult. Some suggested beginnings follow.

- *Dear . . .*

- *I wish I could have a second chance to make things turn out differently.*

- *When I think of you . . .*

- *Please forgive me.*

- *No one can ever take your place in my heart.*

- *I plan to try and help others avoid the mistakes I made.*

- *Though all must die some time, in some way, your death came too soon.*

- *I hope you are at peace with God.*

- *I love you and hope to see you again when my time comes.*

Write whatever you think would be meaningful to the deceased, and write assuming s/he can know what you are writing. Revise as many times as you wish. It may be useful to read them over and over until full recognition of the difference between excuses and responsibility has been assimilated. These notes are very personal, yet powerful. When finished, you might want to destroy your notes. Writing is for *you*, to face what is in your heart, to accept your own human limitations and errors, and then to move on. Long-term suffering has little value. You cannot change the past, but there is a great deal you can do to positively affect the future – both yours and others.

5) Killing in the line of duty.

During a war, miscalculation or misinformation causes unintentional deaths, both of innocent civilians or one's own troops. Others cannot imagine what profound sorrow this causes to whomever pulled the trigger or dropped the bomb.

When killing is done under orders, and only enemy die, many military personnel still regret the necessity for taking another's life. Guilt can ensue for a long time.

As a police or security officer, you sometimes must kill in the line of duty. Though some departments provide psychological or psychiatric counseling, few opt to avail themselves of this service for fear that their professional image will be compromised. I hope this is changing. Meanwhile, *private writing* to the deceased may help soften the unhappy memory. Destroy the note when you have finished.

- *To . . .*
- *Maybe it shouldn't bother me that I had to . . . but it does.*
- *I wish you hadn't . . .*
- *I don't know what in your life caused you to be where you were . . .*
- *I hope your family doesn't suffer too much . . .*
- *Forgive me for doing what I had to do.*

6) Gang murder or homicide while engaged in a crime.

Conscience, the awareness and urge to do right and not wrong can be suppressed when under the influence of alcohol, drugs, or a feared/respected person. Maybe your conscience was warped to the point that you thought it was *right* to kill. If your conscience has begun operating properly, you now feel sincere regret. That will probably always be with you, but the sharp edges of remorse can be dulled.

Privately write a note to your deceased victim/s. Some ideas on how to begin follow.

· *When I shot, stabbed, etc. you, I thought . . .*
· *I was . . . years old.*
· *What I was trying to do was to . . .*
· *I now feel very sorry for what I did.*
· *If I had known then what I know now, I never would have . . .*
· *Please forgive me.*
· *I hope your family doesn't suffer too much.*

A part of healing from our past mistakes is to find some way to forgive ourselves. A formal confession to a spiritual advisor, and asking forgiveness from God, may bring some relief. If possible and feasible, ask forgiveness from others effected by the death.

Ultimately, we must forgive ourselves for our past mistakes if we are to pursue the most meaningful lives. It can be quite useful to write a letter to yourself – your *younger guilty* self – and when finished, destroy it. It is for you only, a *private writing.*

- *Dear younger self – Dear guilty self – Dear young Max . . .*
- *When you killed . . . you thought . . .*
- *You were influenced by . . .*
- *Now, I, as the older you, know and understand it was wrong.*
- *I forgive you, young Max.*

Many former gang members or criminals have matured, and become responsible citizens. You can too. Consider using your experience to educate others. You might offer safety lectures in schools, or assist in a program designed to inform and protect others from becoming victims.

7) Guilt for being alive.

Feeling guilt for still being alive is not uncommon. Reasons include:

- Someone died while trying to do something for you.

· One or more of your comrades died in military or police combat.

If you feel guilty because someone else died instead of you, write to him/her expressing what you think and feel. It can be a step in being able to re-claim your right to be alive. Some ideas in how to begin your letter follow.

· *Dear . . .*

· *Your death affected me deeply.*

· *What I remember of our time together is . . .*

· *I am trying to come to grips with all the circumstances around what happened.*

· *When I think if only this, or if only that, it doesn't help my state of mind.*

· *Please forgive me if any of my choices hastened your death.*

· *I will try to live my life in a way you approve.*

· *I love you.*

For some, consultation with a spiritual advisor may be necessary to begin a release.

> *A Vietnam veteran, at the insistence of his wife, sought help for his anguish and guilt over a buddy who died in the war. None of my efforts were fruitful; he was unable to*

> *say or write what happened. After he found*
> *a wise and compassionate priest to whom*
> *he confessed whatever it was, he began to*
> *have relief.*

It is defeating to spend too much energy chastising ourselves. Regardless of what happened, the only benefit in suffering over it is whatever lessons may be learned. Once that is done, the next step is to write a letter to yourself. Guilty grief is almost impossible to eradicate until we forgive ourselves for our human deficits. Give yourself the loving understanding you would try to extend to a friend suffering the same way.

- *Dear self . . .*
- *I accept your humanity with all its limitations, as all people must.*
- *I forgive you for your ignorance, arrogance, poor choices, etc.*
- *I see potential for doing good in this world.*
- *I will try to help others, even if in a small way, every chance I get.*
- *From this experience I have learned . . .*
- *Through my own grief, I will extend compassion to others suffering grief.*

- *I believe it is your duty to go on with the life* God gave you.
- *I give you permission to find peace of mind.*

Write encouraging letters to yourself whenever you start sinking into fruitless recrimination, and think of ways to make a difference in the lives of others. It can be useful to write a forgiving letter to yourself, and then mail it back to yourself.

If you consider homicide or suicide, please call your local help line or seek professional help. Thousands of people have found their way out of grief and depression to a life of peace and joy. You can too. More death is not the solution to grief.

All of us are developmental, and whatever wisdom comes to us is often through suffering. Following any tragedy, with or without our personal culpability in its happening, we best ask ourselves what we can learn from the experience, and how we can live more lovingly (discussed more fully in *Part V: Reinvesting in Love*).

PART IV:
REMEMBERING JOY

Marilyn J. Walker, PH.D

Chapter 13:
Sweet Moments & Fun

Human propensity to find joy takes many forms. We can delight in simple pleasures of taste, touch and sight. Music can enthrall us, physical achievement invigorate us, and an unexpected turn of phrase make us laugh. Remembering past joy helps us to re-live it anew.

One of my nephews was killed at age twelve by a youthful driver whose car swerved into his yard. My brother's anguish was etched on his face as he stroked the face of his beloved son in the casket. His wife was still in shock; her grief was to come to the fore later on. Immediately before and after the funeral, she engaged in sweet memories, and recounted to us the cute things he had done, the anecdotes which had brought them pride and joy.

Following the death of a loved one, most of us are too immersed in grief to remember the joy. My sister-in-law's sorrow upon losing her precious son was deep, and her joyful memories of her son's life so soon after his death is unusual. Eventually though, as we recover from the grief of loss, it is one of the healthiest things we can do. If asked if we'd rather s/he had never been born," for people we have loved, the answer is most likely, "no." We valued and enjoyed them and are glad to have been able to share in their lives as long as we did. A second question is, do you believe the deceased would *want* you to grieve or suffer endlessly over their death? This isn't likely. So think back and write as much as you can remember about the sweet moments and fun.

- S/he was born in . . . on the date of . . .
- What made him/her laugh.
- Outings, vacations . . .
- I'll never forget the time . . .
- Gifts s/he gave or received.
- Best friends.
- Preferred foods.
- Funny things said, jokes, tricks.
- What I loved most about him/her was . . .
- S/he was happiest when . . .
- About singing, s/he . . .
- Other.

Chapter 14: Aspirations, Successes & Dreams

Working toward a goal and entertaining dreams for the future are some of life's greatest pleasures. Even though very few achieve all of what we wish, the pursuit brings satisfaction. Aspirations, successes and dreams of the deceased are to be cherished, because along with whatever love came his/her way, they were the spice of life. Try to recall what you can in chronological order: as an infant, toddler, elementary school child, junior high, high school, college, adulthood, middle age, senior citizen. If you find yourself smiling as you write, you are capturing the essence of his/her life and showing appreciation for it through your memories.

- S/he was interested in . . .
- Obstacles or handicaps s/he overcame, or functioned in spite of.
- S/he was so proud when . . .
- Special talents s/he hoped to . . .
- Wanted to become a . . .
- Graduated from . . .
- Actually became a . . .

- · Received recognition for . . .
- · Other.

Death awaits us all, but grieving over that fact detracts from remembering the aspirations, successes and dreams our loved ones enjoyed. Focusing on such memories when we think of loved ones that have gone on before us can help us to accept their death, and remind us that their lives were meaningful. Then we'd best focus on our own aspirations and take whatever steps we can to realize them. Such sweet efforts imbue our lives with meaning, and keep us from a living death years before our time.

PART V:
REINVESTING
IN LOVE

Marilyn J. Walker, PH.D .

PART V:

REINVESTING IN LOVE

Love takes many forms. It may be a deep, tender feeling of affection toward a child, parent or other relative; admiration of friends or public figures; or an attraction which includes a desire for intimacy and romance. For some, sex alone constitutes love. Emotional attachment to a pet is a special kind of love. Enthusiasm for a treasured object or property; or for certain activities – travel, sports, the outdoors, etc. may be expressed as love. After a loss, reinvestment in love can bring solace and healing.

Marilyn J. Walker, PH.D

Chapter 15: The Risks

1) Romantic love.

The hurt that underlies grief can trigger a protective reaction to shield us from future pain. Avoidance of attachments or love is such a mechanism. Check the risks below that have occurred to you:

· Another loss at some point.

· Guilt for loving someone else.

· Disapproval of family members.

· The costs – financial or emotional – could outweigh the benefits.

· Risk of rejection if you try.

· Being exploited in some way.

· Could never find someone as good as . . .

· Might get someone worse than the last one.

· You are self-sufficient, don't want to give up freedom or independence.

· Made a death-bed promise to dying mate never to love anyone else.

Love of another does not expect such a

sacrifice. Wise people's minds change, and loving again is not a betrayal.

· Other.

2) **Association with others.**

Reinvestment in love need not entail a romantic partner. Options to join others in an honorable endeavor or for social activities are limitless. It is necessary, however, that one put forth the effort to make such connections, and be willing to overcome minor risks. What might prevent you from trying?

· Not being warmly accepted.

· Having to deal with the foibles and idiosyncrasies of others.

· Transportation problems.

· Other.

3) **Isolation.**

Having alone time is healthy. Being alone *all the time,* though, is not. Without interaction with others, we tend to become depressed, or develop a kind of cynicism. Many now connect with others through a computer – e-mail, chat rooms, on-line games, or other internet venues. You must be cautious, however. Predators also use the internet to find lonely people to exploit financially or physically. Do not reveal your finances or address, and promise nothing. If you want to meet someone, only do so in a public place, making sure a friend or family member knows with whom and where. Preferably take someone else along with you. Also, the phone is a great way to reach out.

> *Mrs. J. is an invalid, confined to her bed most of the time. Her daughter-in-law says of her, "Entering her room is always a bright spot in my day. She spends her time phoning other shut-ins to cheer them up. She is the most positive person I know."*

Consider the benefits of reinvesting in love listed below, and think about participation in a church, a singles club, or any other group that might pique your interest, given a chance.

Marilyn J. Walker, PH.D

Chapter 16:
The Benefits

1) Intimacy.

Wanting to be loved is a basic longing for most of us. Romantic love, when it is found, brings benefits.

- You are not alone.

- Feeling of being loved.

- Improved physical and mental health.

- Reduction in depression, a common problem among older people and those who live alone.

- Companionship.

- Someone with whom to discuss ideas.

- Sexual satisfaction.

- Shared duties: home and financial.

- Partner for outings, travel.

2) Interaction with others.

If we do not wish to pursue romantic love, we still need love in our lives. Consider:

- Becoming closer to family members: children, parents, aunts, uncles, cousins, nieces or nephews. Invite them over; ask about their lives. Love them. One or more of them are likely to love you back.

- Joining others in an honorable endeavor. Schools need volunteers. Thousands of children need foster care. Most churches will welcome you. Political organizations abound that represent whatever values you hold.

- Attending support group meetings to share your grief with others who also mourn.

  These can be found through hospitals, social services, churches or the yellowpages.

- Participate in social activities. Invite a neighbor over for coffee. Find a bridge group, a tennis partner or a chat room on the internet.

- Get a pet that will love you back.

Yes, death has touched you, as it touches us all, Now though, it is important to live as fully and lovingly as you can. Write away your hurts, regrets, grievances, and angers. Record the joy and sweet memories, and as you do, remember that love is contagious. Living lovingly enriches our own lives as well as those around us. If someone reaches out to you, respond appreciatively. If need be, *you* reach out.

Addendum:

Letters Written to Deceased Loved Ones

The following letters include remembered joy, regrets, and whatever else the writers wanted to say. Although it may take years for one to discover how writing can be a relief, when undertaken, it is a powerful catharsis. Stable intelligent persons wrote the following letters and agreed to let them be published in this book.

Marilyn J. Walker, PH.D

1) A mom writes to her beloved son

Dear Kevin,

It has been years since you were taken from us, yet it still seems like yesterday. It's amazing to look back over time and reflect on the variety of emotions that we experienced as we tried to deal with your loss.

One Monday night you talked to your dad and I on the phone, making us laugh for 45 minutes while you gave us a blow-by-blow account of the basketball game your team lost. A few hours later, someone else called to tell us you were dead. To learn the horror of your death at the hands of a drunk driver, and to learn your two teammates died with you, was almost more than we could take.

My memories of the following long months come and go, racing around in my head like a frantic bird in a cage. I remember scores of people coming and going. I remember your friends staying here for days, spending hours telling funny "Kevin stories," and I remember stepping over their sleeping forms at night when I paced the floors.

I listened when someone carefully explained the "stages of grief" to me, but I found they do not occur in numerical order. Some recur with regularity and others simply haunt me forever. I felt unreasonable guilt over not protecting my child. Absolute blind rage that someone could so callously end your life at just 26 years was consuming. Crying jags seemed to go on forever. I recall screaming at God for taking you and screaming at you for leaving me. Over all was the emptiness, the hole in my heart I knew would never go away. Most of all I just miss you with my entire being.

Instead of drawing our family together, our grief often kept us apart. Sometimes when I wanted your dad to hold me while I cried, I would see that he was having a peaceful moment I didn't want to interrupt. He told me he had the same experience. Your poor dad – losing "his" son, born on his birthday, dropped him to his knees. He really never bothered to fight his cancer after you were gone. I think he just decided he would rather be there with you, and he died. I hope the two of you somehow know the fun and laughter you had in this life.

*Your brother has changed since your death –
he's not the big happy teddy bear any more. He still
talks about self-imposed guilt because he was not
there to take care of you, and he still exhibits such
terrible rage toward the person who took you. He
can't sustain a relationship, and his health is suffering. He does have two beautiful little girls that I
wish you and your dad were here to spoil – both of
you were so foolish about little kids.*

*As for me, I guess I will always remain the crazy
lady I have become. I love to wear an item of your
clothing – it feels like a hug. I will always sleep
with the little stuffed elephant toy you brought me
from one of your trips; the little tag he wears that
says, "Don't forget I love you" means so much. I
sometimes smell you when I enter a room. I hear
your voice in my head. Every now and then some
unknowing person will tell me I should get on
with my life. Well, I have. I function. I took care of
your dad. I go to work and do the laundry and
shop for groceries. But some people don't understand that one can "go on" but can never "get
over" the death of a child.*

I want to thank you for being such an extraordinary person. You were a total joy as a child, a terrific teenager, and a great friend as a young man. You were so handsome, so bright, so talented – I am so proud to be your mom. You lived more in your 26 years than most people could in a hundred, and I thank you for living so well.

It's strange to be writing you a letter. Since I talk to you every day, I sense you know all this. I feel your presence, your love, and it's a great comfort.

As I tell you every night, "Fly, son. Know peace and joy, and don't forget I love you."

Mom

2) A grown son's extraordinary letter to his father

Dear Dad,

Remember when you died, Dad? Did you know that I was the only one in the room with you as you were making those awful noises? You were in the big bed at the windows – I was on a cot over by the wall. Mom came out of the bathroom. She was about ready to leave for church. I asked her, "Is something wrong with Daddy?" And that's how we began to experience your dying and your death. You were 47. I was 10.

Mom wiped your face with a damp wash cloth, and she said, "Johnny? Johnny?" But you wouldn't respond. Later she asked an ambulance person or policeman, "Is he dead?" And Mom cried when the response was affirmative.

You know, Dad, I didn't cry a lot about things. . . but I cried at least three times anyway after you died. Once was when the hearse came to pick up your body. I was looking out the window from the room in which you died. Then a neighbor man came over. He sort of put his hands on me and pulled me up close and talked about how sad it was to lose your daddy. I didn't want to cry but I did.

And then at the funeral in the chapel Nancy cried and I felt so mad at her because she was making me cry too. Remember the caisson, dad? That was really something – horse drawn. I've never been back there. I'll go over there some time Dad.

You know, Dad, it's strange but I never really felt you were a great influence on my life. I mean, after you died, I never gave you much thought. It's like your life – and your death – really weren't very meaningful or important to me. Of course I have been aware for years . . . have memories of so many events – traumatic and revolving around you and your alcoholism. We called it drunkenness then, if it was talked about at all. You know what I'm talking about? Like the time you had mom backed against the wall and us three kids were on the stairs watching. But Henry had the 22 rifle and made you leave mom alone.

Now, Dad, wasn't that a hell of a thing to subject your family to? Do you – did you ever think

about how I was affected by such shenanigans?
You know, I remember that event and others, but I
don't recall my feelings about them. Wouldn't you
think I'd remember being scared, or something? . . .

Isn't it something, Dad, as awful as that and the
other experiences were, we <u>never</u>, <u>never</u> talked about
them. It's as if it were a humdrum event that wasn't
of interest to anyone.

But I'm in ACA (Adult Children of Alcoholics)
now Dad. Sure has been helpful to me. For the first
time, I understand rather clearly why I turned out as
I did and it opened doors to positive changes in my
life. I think Alcoholics Anonymous was well off the
ground back then. Too bad you couldn't take advan-
tage of it, Dad. I'll bet you were pretty depressed –
probably just couldn't handle it is my guess. So
despite what I said about subjecting us to those bad
experiences, I'm not writing this to condemn or
judge you, Dad, but just to clear the air, to say it's
OK; I understand, and I'm sorry. Sorry that you
couldn't get it all together and there seemed no way
out (I'm trying to understand it all).

You know, you really weren't such a bad guy. I

mean you weren't diabolical; you never planned bad things for the family and others. I know you would have liked being a positive influence for others. I remember you played the violin, and you sang, "It's Only a Shanty in Old Shanty Town." That's still a favorite tune for me.

I've felt that my childhood was all bad . . . but I guess it wasn't _all_ bad. I remember your upholstering a chair. Remember the boat you made for me? You made such great boats with tackle and steam pipes and moving parts. I had felt self-pity because you had made some boats for others and I wanted one. I was sitting out on the back porch, pouting. I had thought that I would make my own boat since you hadn't made me one. Of course it was a sham. I had no idea how to go about it. But you saw me sad and pouting and you made me a nice boat. Also, it was kind of nice to go with you to our garden at least once.

One really good thing you did for me was to get me that cat – Whitey. I had her for many years. I recall we went over to the farmer to get her as a kitten, and you said, "Much obliged." She died *many years later, after you died, as she delivered dead kittens. I think by then I had learned to repress feelings and I didn't feel terribly sad.*

I'll tell you though, Dad, when Mom died, I cried, first at home. But at the funeral service I really let it out. I cried loud and hard and long. It was a desperate crying – revealing my lostness, my helplessness, my not knowing, my frustration, my need to be loved and to love, my alienation from even those closest to me. I've sure had a miserable life, Dad. Up until now, that is.

In all fairness, Dad, I have so many resources of help that you and Mom never had – a wealth of self-help books, Adult Children of Alcoholics, psycho-therapy, support groups. I'm so much better off financially than you and Mom ever were. I'm not so locked into rigid beliefs that may have limited you. I've got a good job, look forward to retirement in a few years . . . and to increased knowledge, aware-ness and growth. . . . I think I can be a positive force, yet, for others.

I tell you what, Dad, I'm glad I'm alive – glad that you and Mom "had" me; but you know, in ACA, we see God as our real parent. No offense, but really, God is our real father/mother. . . . I suppose all families are dysfunctional to some extent, and that ideal parenting is maybe never attained, and that's OK when we see God as our real parent.

Understanding my childhood family is extremely meaningful and liberating for me. It doesn't matter that I'm "arriving" at a rather late time in my life. I'm alive, and the journey is interesting. I'm more accepting of whatever the results are. But also, I like the idea that the essence of my being is spiritual, in love – and I want to nurture that reality.

Well, Dad, maybe you have a means of communicating with me. I'm receptive to the idea. If so, let me "hear" from you.

Love, Charles

P.S. They don't call me "Charlsie" anymore. Welcome back into my life, Dad.

3) A daughter writes regrets and sweet memories to her mother

Dear Sweet Mom,

I remember when we lived in that 2-story house with a basement and some kittens had been born there. I must have been four or five years old. You were busy as usual sorting fruit for canning or something. You accidentally stepped on one of the kittens and it died. You felt so awful. The cat living in my house is constantly running under my feet and I once accidentally stepped on her foot and another time on her tail. I understand how easily it can happen.

How impressionable we are as children. Once you ridiculed me when I was watching you nurse my baby brother. The ridicule was very hurtful. I'm sure now that you had no idea how much such remarks can wound the ego of a little kid and would not do it intentionally.

I remember you helping me with schoolwork. I can still see you baking pies and making pancakes. You protected two of my sisters from daddy's fists when he was angry, putting yourself between them and him.

Mostly I remember a happy childhood: mountain climbing, lots of Sunday company for dinner, pitching horseshoes, and sitting on the front porch swapping stories with uncles. I had freedom to play in the vacant lots on both sides of our house and could walk to the hilltop park with friends. Things have changed so much that parks aren't so safe anymore.

I want you to know two particular regrets I have. When you were living with me and I was teaching during the day, after work I would sink down on the couch facing the one where you were without really talking to you. One day you asked me if I was mad at you. I said, "No. I'm just tired." But in looking back, if I had had more understanding of how lonely you were, there by yourself all day, no doubt anticipating having some company, I would have handled it differently. I should have shared some of what had happened during my day, and asked what was on your mind. I can't believe how ignorant I was.

I tried to see that you got the best of care, like when I took you out of that "home" that had such

inept and uncaring staff, and placed you in a Chris-
tian home where you were happy. I took you on
outings, and visited you regularly. We took picnic
lunches to the lake, and to the park to watch the
ducks. We went on drives by the river.

As you developed a mild dementia, you some-
times accused me of stealing your clothes when I
took them to launder for you, or said other things
that hurt me. One day when I was particularly
stressed, I cried and said I didn't think you loved me.
You looked so shocked, confused and hurt.
Now that I am more mature, I realize what an awful
thing that was to say. You dedicated your whole life
to being the best wife and mother you could. Of
course you made mistakes as we all do. Once I
heard you talking on the phone, talking about me
with pride, something you never said to me, always
fearing one of us would get the "big head." Guess
what? I got it anyway. Am over it now.

But at the end of your life to hear from a daugh-
ter that she thought you didn't love her must have
been a terrible blow. I didn't mean to be cruel, and
at the time didn't realize that it was. I was caught up

Marilyn J. Walker, PH.D

in my own hurts, problems, and worries. Please forgive me. I know you loved me.

I was so proud of you in the retirement home. You dressed up each day and looked great. You entertained the other residents with your singing and poetry. You were a natural talent; no wonder you were chosen to act for the TV commercial. Your wit and sense of humor was part of why you became buddies with the chaplain who adored you. After you died he wrote me a letter, saying that it was always hard to lose a resident, but some losses were harder than others. He missed you.

You were a wonderful mom. All of your children still miss you and love you. We talk about your specific teachings that continue to influence us. Thank you.

I often wish I could visit with you just one more time as you were before the dementia took place. I'm glad though that your travails are over and that you have no more confusion and pain. As my life encounters more – shall I say – challenges, I appreciate you more and more as the years go by.

Love, just me

Readings:

A Grief Observed, C.S. Lewis, Bantam Doubleday Dell, Feb. 1976. When he lost his wife, the love of his life, to breast cancer, he addressed his overwhelming grief by writing about it.

Angels, God's Secret Agents, Billy Graham, Doubleday & Company, Inc., Garden City, New York. 1975. Reviews some of the 300 references to angels mentioned in the Bible.

Closer to the Light, Melvin Morse, M.D., with Paul Perry, Villard Books, New York 1990. Research studies of Near Death Experiences of children, with glimpses of the afterlife.

Death is of Vital Importance. Elisabeth Kubler-Ross, M.D., Compiled & Edited by Goran Grip, M.D., Station Hill Press, Inc., Barrytown, NY, 1995. On Life, Death, and Life After Death.

Embraced by the Light, Betty J. Eadie, Gold Leaf Press, 2533 North Carson St. Suite 1544, Carson City, NV, 89706, 1992. Account of her Near Death Experience and the love and beauty on the other side.

<u>Gentle Closings, How to Say Goodbye to Someone You Love</u>, Ted Menten, Running Press, Philadelphia, Pa., 1991.

<u>Giving Sorrow Words</u>, Candy Lightner (Founder of MADD, Mothers Against Drunk Driving) & Nancy Hathaway, Warner Books,NY, 1990.

<u>Life at Death, </u>, Kenneth Ring, Ph.D., Coward, McCann & Gerghegan, New York, 1980. A Scientific Investigation of the Near Death Experience.

<u>Man's Search for Meaning,</u> Victor E. Frankl, M.D., 1905-1997. Written while a prisoner in German Nazi concentration camps. Pocket Books, New York, 1939,1963.

<u>On Children and Death</u>, Elisabeth Kubler-Ross, M.D., MacMillan Publishing Co., New York, 1983.

<u>On Death and Dying</u>, Elisabeth Kubler-Ross, M.D., MacMillan Publishing Co., Inc., New York, 1969. What the dying have to teach doctors, nurses, clergy and their own families.

<u>Start the Conversation</u>, Ganga Stone, Warner Books, New York, 1996. Philosophy and evidence that there is no such thing as death.